CHICAGO

Text by
RICHARD FREMANTLE

Photos by
ANDREA PISTOLESI

BONECHI

Distributed by

Karina Wang
PhotoScapes
565 Drexel Avenue
Glencoe, Illinois 60022
Tel/Fax (708) 8352941

© Copyright 1995 by CASA EDITRICE BONECHI
Via Cairoli, 18/b 50131 Firenze - Italy
Telex 571323 CEB - Fax 055/5000766

Photo Credits
Photographs from the Archives of Casa Editrice Bonechi
taken by ANDREA PISTOLESI.

The two pictures on page 43 (Photo Gamma) were
provided by the ILLINOIS BUREAU OF TOURISM *that the*
Publisher thanks for the cooperation in the production of this book.

Text by RICHARD FREMANTLE

Printed in Italy by
Centro Stampa Editoriale Bonechi

Sole Agent in North America:
Ilaria Sartori
255 Centre Street
6th Floor
New York, NY 10013
Tel/Fax (212) 343-1464

ISBN 88-7009-887-7

* * *

The Chicago River in downtown Chicago. To the far left
is the **Hancock Building**, in the left foreground the
Chicago Sun-Times building, straight ahead the **Wrigley
Building** and on the right, the **Equitable Building**.

CHICAGO IS AMERICA'S HEART!

When you gaze down from the **Sears** or **Hancock
Towers** onto the enormous prairie city of over
seven million people which spreads westward
from Lake Michigan, you are looking at
America's heart. New York is the mid-point
between the Atlantic world and the United States.
San Francisco is the similar mid-point between
the Pacific world and America. But what you see
below you when you look down on Chicago is the
mid-point of the whole of America itself, not just
from east to west but from north to south, the mid-
point of the North American continent.
What started only a hundred and fifty years ago
as a tiny trading community, is now the hub of
modern commercial and cultural spokes that lead
from the Arctic down to South America, from
New York to San Francisco, from Alaska to the
West Indies, from Newfoundland to Mexico.
O'Hare's place as the world's busiest airport is
an index of this position, and the recent Canada-
U.S. Trade Agreement an affirmation of its future.
Chicago not only stands on the extremity of the
eastern United States, at the beginning of the
western prairies, it's at the southern edge of the
Great Lakes System which joins the northern part
of the American continent to the south, and vice-
versa, the south to the north.
Chicago is literally America's heart, for more of
America's energy is concentrated in and near
Chicago than anywhere else. If you look southwest from the top of your skyscraper, just a few
miles, maybe six or seven, towards Midway
airport, to where the south branch of the Chicago
River becomes narrow, you will be looking at the
spot, a tiny magic link, from which grew
everything you see below you.
Even from long before Europeans appeared, that
spot was known and appreciated as the minute
link between the Great Lakes - Saint Lawrence
River water system, which flows into the Atlantic
over 1,000 miles to the east, and the Missouri -
Mississippi River system which spreads
throughout the whole of mid-America between
the Appalachians and the Rockies, to flow into
the Gulf of Mexico about 1,000 miles to the south.
For unknown scores of generations before
French explorers and traders first found the spot
in the 17th century, the Indians knew that by
carrying their canoes a few thousand yards west
from where the south branch of the Chicago

3

*A magnificent panorama of central Chicago masts of the many pleasure craft anchored in the **Marina**. To the left, is the **Sears Tower**, and to the right, the **John Hancock Building**. In the center are the diamond-shaped **Associates Center**, the **Prudential Building**, and the tall, white **Amoco Building** to their right. Near the **Hancock Building** are the Bloomingdale Building, Water Tower Place and Harbour Point.*

River rises, near Leavitt Avenue today, across the slight elevation there, to the Des Plaines River, at about 49th and Harlem, they could travel by water almost anywhere over and around the whole American continent east of the Rockies.

European immigrants quickly understood the same magic of that spot. As long as they went no farther west than Chicago, they could retain their European origins. The water route back East was always there to tie them to their roots. But the moment they crossed that little rise and started west across the prairies, they became American. They entered an Indian world, a pioneer world, a world where nature had always, from time immemorial, dominated man and equalized him, and not man nature, as they had known in Europe.

BLUE COLLAR

Chicago is a blue collar city, a working man's town. It wasn't founded, like the East by educated colonists who left Europe for religious freedom or financial gain.
It was built up on the backs of waves of immigrants, most of whom were not only uneducated but who didn't even speak English. These people came to the city which grew into the world's most important commercial crossroads and entrepôt, in search of work. They made Chicago.
While there are plenty of rich people in Chicago, there is no aristocracy. If you're not willing to work, and hard, you're not really part of the city. All the glories of the *Art Institute* - and they are

*The **Wrigley Building** seen from the opposite bank of the Chicago River - built in 1931.*

*The **Wrigley Building**, and the **Tribune Tower**, built in 1925, Chicago's two classic downtown office buildings.*

*The two separate blocks of the **Wrigley Building**, with the **IBM Regional Center** behind to the left.*

magnificent glories - are really just a solitary imported peak of Chicago's cultural mountain. The Art Institute contains mostly other people's art: East Coast, European and Oriental. Chicago's own arts are Blues and Jazz, Architecture, Business, Contemporary theater and, above all else, Lifestyle.

Chicago is before all other towns, *the* quintessential American city, a great inland port on the western-most edge of America's enormous continental inland sea, a city full of parks, surrounded by the most delightful continent of them all — America!

It's the County Town for the whole of middle America - the center of the most productive agricultural and industrial area on the whole planet, and as such the core of America's strength. Carl Sandburg also called it 'the city of big shoulders'.

HISTORY

The word Chicago seems to have been an Indian name for a strong-smelling onion which grew in the muddy flats at the River's mouth. 'We went in canoes on the river Chicagou...' wrote a Jesuit missionary, Henri de Tonti, in 1681 - an unprepossessing beginning for such a magnificent development.

There is a strong possibility that the Vikings, around the year 1,000 or even earlier, found the Saint Lawrence River and followed it into the Great Lakes, crossing them to Lake Michigan. But the first Europeans we know to have visited the site of Chicago were Louis Jolliet and Jacques Marquett, two Frenchmen, in 1673.

Whereas the English settled directly along the eastern seaboard of the United States, the French had travelled from Newfoundland up the Saint

The Clock Tower of the **Wrigley Building** *and a detail of the upper part of the Wrigley Building's northern tower.*

The **Wrigley Building**, *the* **Tribune Tower**, *and the* **Equitable Building** *at night, seen from the South bank of the Chicago River.*

Lawrence, and established forts at Quebec and Montreal. It was natural for them to explore farther along the river, trading with the Indians, crossing the Great Lakes, to arrive eventually at the southern end of Lake Michigan, and at the mouth of the Chicago River. From there, led by local Indian guides, they had only to cross the short portage at the source of the Chicago River, to enter the Illinois and Mississippi River tributaries. From there they were able to travel westwards by water all the way to the Rockies, or south to what became New Orleans, and into the Gulf of Mexico.

In 1763 the French lost the Seven Years War to the British. With it they lost most of their American territory. For about twenty years the area around Chicago's River was claimed by the British. After the American Revolution, the British

A view of Chicago's heart at night. From the left: the **Quaker Oats Building**, *the* **Chicago Sun-Times Building**, *the* **Wrigley Building**, *the* **Tribune Tower** *just visible behind, and the* **Equitable Building**.

colonists who had won their independence from England, began colonizing as Americans, and immediately claimed it was theirs. The Indians of course knew all along that it really belonged to them, so in 1812 they massacred most of the occupants of the original - illegal - Fort Dearborn, which had been established at the mouth of the Chicago River.

As long as the Indians continued to claim and defend their territory, there was no development of the area by Europeans. In the early 1830's the native Americans were finally chased westwards, and that's when Chicago begins.

The town was incorporated in 1833 with a population of about three hundred and fifty people. Its river harbor was improved the following year, with a deepened channel at its mouth, and 500 foot-long piers on either side.

CHICAGO'S GROWTH AND TWO CANALS

Chicago's growth was prodigious. Perhaps never before in the whole history of man has a city grown so fast and so magnificently. Within a hundred years Chicago had increased ten thousand times from its 350 people, to three-and-a-half million people. It had also gone from being a tiny trading establishment, to being the center of an area of production, service and manufacturing without equal on the face of the earth.

"Make no little plans: they have no magic to stir men's blood...
Make big plans, aim high and hope and worth, remembering that a noble logical diagram once recorded will never die...

*The Gothic top of the **Chicago Tribune Tower**, by night and by day, showing its ornamental piers and flying buttresses, and a detail of the top portion of the **Chicago Tribune Tower**, seen from the Michigan Ave. Bridge across the Chicago River.*

*The **Chicago Tribune Tower**, built in 1925 after an international competition produced this magnificent proposal.*

Remember that our sons and grandsons are going to do things that would stagger us..."
Daniel H. Burnham, architect of the 1909 Plan of Chicago

Together with the arrival of the railroads, it was the opening of two canals which made the city so important.
Before the Erie Canal opened in 1825, the easiest route west was across the Appalachians, and then once on their western slopes, from Pittsburg to Cleveland on Lake Erie or along the Ohio River to Cincinnati, Louisville, Evansville, and to the Mississippi.
With the opening of the Erie Canal it was possible to travel by water from New York City to Buffalo, and then across the Great Lakes to Chicago.
From 1825 onwards, the fates of New York and Chicago as the largest and most vital American

cities were joined.
Then in 1848 the *Illinois and Michigan Canal* finally opened, joining the Chicago and Des Plaines Rivers, and with them the waters of the north Atlantic and the Gulf of Mexico.
This canal was the magic link which everyone had wanted from the moment the first settlers arrived in Chicago. They knew it assured forever the city's commercial and entrepreneurial supremacy in the mid-continent.
From 1850 onwards the expansion of Chicago as by far the most important railroad center in America's westward expansion meant that a large part of America's produce was handled and processed in the city, and that an enormous part of all manufacture either took place in Chicago or near it, or at least had to pass through the city.

A detail of the statue of **George Washington** *across the Chicago River from Marina City, at Heald Square. This monument was dedicated in 1941. It includes statues of Robert Morris and Haym Salomon, two bankers who helped finance the American Revolution.*

Ornamental figures from the recently restored **Wacker Drive Fountain**.

The **Clark Street Bridge** over the Chicago River. In the
background to the left is the Merchandise Mart.

*"The corn crop is condensed and
reduced in bulk by feeding it into an
animal form more portable. The hog eats
the corn and Europe eats the hog. Corn
thus becomes incarnate for what is a hog
but 15 or 20 bushels of corn on four
legs?"*

Unknown commentator on Chicago's
stockyards.

CHICAGO'S DEVELOPMENT

Our romantic movie and TV view of the West in
the 19th century is one of Cowboys and Indians,
gunslingers and sheriffs. But the true view is one
of America at work.
Farmers, lumberjacks, cattlemen, sheep-men,
pig-farmers, horse-breeders and team-drivers,
ironsmiths, farriers, coal-miners, warehousemen,
wharfmen, sailors and chandlers, coopers,
carpenters and builders, travelling salesmen,
merchants of every sort, gunsmiths - the true

America was one of work - of the manufacture
and distribution of every tool needed to tame and
settle a Continent - of reapers and their locust-
like movement across hundreds of miles of
prairies, of many kinds of grain, and scores of
every imaginable agricultural product being
handled in Chicago to be shipped back East and
to Europe.
At different times in its short history Chicago has
been a lumber capital, a milling, and a wood-
furniture capital, a grain capital, a farm machine
and tool capital, a printing capital, a capital for
textiles, for breweries, for the slaughtering of
animals, for meat-packing, and for tanning, for
mail-order merchandising, for shopping centers,
for steel, and especially for railroads and for
Pullman sleeping cars, for the film industry, a
capital for what today is called venture finance.
It's always been a capital for building, for
architecture, and for real estate speculation. It
was even, as we all know so well, a bootlegging
and gangster capital. Chicago is a city built upon
the backs of working men. Even the gangsters
depended on them...

One of the sightseeing boats which ply the Chicago River and Lake Michigan in the summer, seen from the **Wacker Drive Bridge** over the Chicago River.

Two details of the ornaments on the **Wacker Drive Bridge**.

IMMIGRATION

Where did they come from, those working men? First of all, in the 1840's, from Ireland, fleeing the potato failures. The Irish immigrant influence has always been important in Chicago's workforce, in its politics and government.
Then after the failed social uprisings of the late 1840's in the Austrian Empire, Austrians and Germans arrived in large numbers.
By the 1860's more than half of the city's population of over 100,000 people was foreign-born.
The Irish and Germans were followed by large numbers of Scandinavians, and smaller numbers of Britons - the Scots, the Welsh and the English. The city grew with Czechs, Hungarians and Slavs, German-speaking Jews, Poles, Dutch, Lithuanians, Latvians and Estonians, with Greeks and with Orientals.

Towards the end of the century and in this one, these large groups were joined by Italians, Russians, Jews from all over Eastern Europe, Armenians, Syrians and, most recently, by Latinos: Spanish-speaking people from everywhere in Latin America, particularly from Puerto Rico and Mexico.
These people made Chicago into the second most ethnically varied city in the United States, where whole neighborhoods were like the immigrants' country of origin, with shops, churches, restaurants and social clubs, with their own newspapers - all just like 'back home'.
The Irish, together with the Germans, Poles, many Czechs, Slovaks and Balts, the Italians, and more recently Latinos, have made Chicago the largest and richest Roman Catholic archdiocese in the world.
Today three of the surviving ethnic enclaves are Greektown, Chinatown, and Ukranian Village.

A section of the 'El' or elevated train, in the **Loop** - a part of downtown Chicago named for this public transport system which 'loops' around it.

After the terrible fire of 1871 all buildings in Chicago had greatly-increased safety features against fire. These brick and reinforced concrete buildings have exterior iron fire-escape stairs.

1871: THE GREAT FIRE IN THE WINDY CITY

Being a city built upon the vast resources of a continent, and developed through the sweat of men's toil, Chicago's history has always had an undercurrent of violence.
Every now and then events occur to remind Chicagoans of this.
Perhaps a sad legacy of those early settlers who died at the Fort Dearborn Massacre, or of the dispossessed native Americans whose lands were taken, this seam of violence re-erupted in extreme racial tension in 1917 and 1918, and then in a vicious five days of riots in 1919. It continued during the '20's when Chicago's gangsters became infamous all over the world.
Even as recently as 1968 serious violence has

reappeared in the Chicago civil riots of that year. By 1870 the growth of the city had been so overwhelming that many Chicagoans saw their city becoming the center of American life. Others, from other cities, jealous, predicted it could not last.
It didn't.
A few minutes past nine on the evening of October 8th, 1871, after an unusually dry spell, a fire started in a Mrs O'Leary's barn just south of the city center. Her house actually survived, as the south wind was strong that evening and the barn was north of the house. But the barn burned, and with it, during the succeeding twenty-four to thirty-six hours, most of Chicago. For about four miles to the north from what is today Taylor, on the south side of the University

*The **Merchandise Mart**, built in 1930, one of the largest merchandising areas in the world.*

*Curved **333 West Wacker Drive**, built in 1983, follows a similar curve in the Chicago River.*

of Illinois campus, to Fullerton in the north, and for about three-quarters of a mile west of Lake Michigan, as far as the north and south branches of the Chicago River, everything was destroyed. Only a few shells of buildings still stood when the fire was over, and the **Water Tower** which still remains as a monument in today's downtown. Some 17,000 buildings burned, leaving 100,000 people homeless - a third of Chicago's population in 1871.

But those who predicted the end of Chicago were wrong.

Like forests which renew themselves through fire, Chicago grew up from its ashes to become even larger and ever more dynamic.

In 1870 the population was about 300,000. By 1880 it was 500,000. By 1900, when a new and much larger canal linking the Chicago and the Des Plaines Rivers, the **Chicago Sanitary and Ship Canal**, was opened, the population was 1.7 million.

By 1920, fifty years after the fire, it was about 3 million.

Chicago had become one of the world's largest cities.

ARCHITECTURE

Any nineteenth century city which grew as fast as Chicago had efficient builders and efficient buildings of every kind — structures adapted continually to the changing needs of people and of trade: warehouses, railroad stations and sheds, piers and wharfs, shipping construction and repair structures, grain storages, factories designed for every purpose, schools, churches, public administration buildings, hospitals, shops, private dwellings.

Both the nearness of abundant timber and the marshiness of Chicago's site, greatly affected Chicago's development of novel building techniques.

The Great Fire of 1871 spurred new building. Chicago became famous and has remained so, for modern architecture.

Almost overnight, after the Fire, Chicago became a brand-new city, making modern inventions like the electric light and the electric elevator commonplace everywhere. In the 1880's William Le Baron Jenney built the first structure, the **Home Insurance Building**, which had both an iron

The **Sears Tower** seen from the **Eisenhower Expressway** before it goes under the **U.S. Post Office Building**. And two of the **Presidential Towers** at 555 W. Madison St.

A view of the **Sears Tower**, showing to its right, the **Bloomingdale Building**, the **Hancock Center**, the **Water Place Tower** and the **First National Bank Building**. In the foreground are the **Chicago River** crossed by the **Jackson Blvd Bridge**, and the **Dwight Eisenhower Expressway** over the **Van Buren St. Bridge**.

and steel-beam skeleton and also a thin exterior non-supporting wall. It was the harbinger of a whole new architecture, to rival the post-and-lintels of the Greeks, and the elegant stone arches of the Romans.
After it, builders realized that there were almost no limits to the potential size and height of buildings. The skyscraper had been born.
Jenney and the other architects of what came to be called 'The Chicago School' - Burnham, Root, Adler and Sullivan - developed a modern architecture in which, against the Victorian tenets of the day, the form of the building was dictated by its function.
This attitude that architecture should be functional was then further expanded and developed by two figures who made Chicago unsurpassed in the history of modern architecture. **Frank Lloyd Wright** (1869-1959), easily the most renowned architect of this

From the top of the **Sears Tower** looking north. **Hancock Center**, the second highest building in Chicago, is flanked on the left by the **Bloomingdale Building**, and on the right by **Water Tower Place**. Beyond is Lake Michigan.

Enjoying the stupendous vistas from the top of the world's highest building - 1454 feet - the **Sears Tower**.

Looking north from the Sears Tower: the **Quaker Oats Building** is in the foreground, **Marina City** and the **IBM Regional Center** in the right foreground. **Hancock Center**, the **Bloomingdale Building**, the **Playboy Club Building**, **Water Tower Place** and **Olympia Center** are all in the center of the picture, with Lake Michigan behind.

*Alexander Calder's large 1974 multi-part mobile in the lobby of the **Sears Tower**, entitled **Universe**. Each of the parts of the mobile moves separately.*

*A view up one side of the world's tallest building, 1454 feet, the **Sears Tower**.*

*Looking west across nightime Chicago towards the praries, from the top of the **Sears Tower**.*

century, had originally worked for Sullivan and Adler, but broke away to build in Oak Park and River Forest alone, some thirty buildings. **Mies van der Rohe** (1886-1969), a German of the Bauhaus School of architecture settled in Chicago in 1938 and built over forty buildings in the city. Frank Lloyd Wright is famous for his private dwellings and for smaller institutional buildings; Mies van der Rohe for skyscrapers.

Over a century has passed since the Great Fire. It has been a period of innovative building in Chicago, and the city is today one of architectural delights. Wooden or stone residences of the 19th and early 20th centuries still charm the eye in parts of the city which were not destroyed by fire. Downtown stone commercial structures of the post - 1871 period survive to set off the shops, corporate buildings and early skyscrapers - structures all built before the Depression years began in 1929.

*The **Chicago Board of Trade** on West Jackson, the world's largest commodities futures trading market - an excitement not to be missed.*

*A typical morning scene at the **Chicago Mercantile Exchange** on South Wacker Drive.*

The post-World War II period - and in particular the last twenty years - has seen great developments in Chicago's architecture. For visitors particularly interested there are many books and guides available, as well as tours both of Frank Lloyd Wright's work, and of the Chicago downtown area.

Many of Chicago's famous buildings are on the National Register of Historic Places, and have been designated with ''Landmark Status'.

The most famous architectural landmarks in Chicago are certainly the **Wrigley Building** of 1921-24 (pp. 6-9) and the **Tribune Tower**, a Gothic Revival gem of 1925 (pp. 10, 11). They stand on either side of Michigan Avenue, just north of the Chicago River, at the beginning of the **Magnificent Mile** - an area of particularly elegant shops. The Wrigley Building was built with money from chewing gum sales, while the Tribune Tower was the result of an international competition to design a new home for one of Chicago's great daily newspapers.

*The central interior of the **State of Illinois Building**, showing the John Henry abstract sculpture, 'Bridgport'.*

*Jean Dubuffet's sculpture outside the **State of Illinois Buildings**, 'Monument with Standing Beast'.*

SCULPTURE

Together with their fine taste in new and beautiful architecture, Chicagoans have one for public sculpture. All over the city are statues and public monuments marking and celebrating moments in the city's and the nation's life.

Older public sculpture and ornament abound. In the downtown area good examples are on the **Wacker Drive Fountain** at Wabash (p. 12), and the **Heald Square Monument** of George Washington flanked by Robert Morris and Haym Salomon, two financial backers of the American Revolution (p. 12), unveiled symbolically as the U.S. entered World War II.

Others are the dramatic fountain monuments of Loredo Taft at the Art Institute, the **Fountain of the Great Lakes** (p. 35) and in Washington Park, called the **Fountain of Time** (p. 62). The **Buckingham Fountain** (p. 42) in Grant Park is one of the largest fountains in the world, 280 feet in diameter, and contains four pairs of bronze

*Some of the many sculptures which adorn the streets of Chicago: top, left and right, Picasso's **Chicago** (1967), between Dearbon and Clark; bottom left, Miro's **Chicago** (1967) in **Brunswick Building Plaza**; bottom right Oldenburg's **Bat Column** (1977) at the **Social Security Administration Building** on West Madison St.; on this page, Calder's **Flamingo** (1974) at **Federal Plaza**, on Dearborn between Adams and Jackson.*

horses representing the four states around Lake Michigan. It was modelled on a similar but smaller fountain at Versailles, in France, and has 133 powerful variable jets of water, which are lit with colored lights at night, making a stunning spectacle.

There are also many new sculptures of contemporary masters commissioned and unveiled in Chicago in recent years: by Picasso, Henry Moore, Mirò, Oldenburg, Chryssa Varda, Richard Lippold, Calder, Marino Marini, Richard Hunt, Louise Nevelson, John Henry, and Jean Dubuffet. These and many others can all be seen inside and outside recent buildings in downtown Chicago.

Fine examples of ornament are also a part of Chicago's architecture and sculptural scene. Particularly famous examples exist on the **Carson Pirie Scott Store** and on the clocks at **Marshall Fields**, both on State Street (pp. 36-37), as well as on the **Wacker Drive Bridge** over the Chicago River (pp. 14-15).

*An aerial view of **Marina City**, the residential and water recreation complex on the north bank of the Chicago River. In the foreground is the **IBM Regional Center**, designed by Mies Van der Rohe. Behind Marina City is the **Quaker Oats Building**, and the Merchandise Mart.*

Marina City, on the north bank of the Chicago River.

CHICAGO'S MAGNIFICENT CONTEMPORARY SKYLINE

The contemporary skyline (pp. 4-5) boasts many recent structures of worldwide reputation: the **Sears Tower** (pp. 20, 21, 24), modern symbol of Chicago's merchandising might, the marble-clad **Amoco Building** (pp. 43, 45) and the **Hancock Center** (pp. 22-23) are three of the tallest buildings in the world. The **Sears** is the tallest of all, at 1454 feet. All have absolutely stupendous views of the city, Lake Michigan, the suburbs, and country-side around the city.

Other famous buildings on the skyline are the **First National Bank Building** (p. 20), and in front of that, with a pyramid-shaped roof, the **Britannica Building** (p. 47). The **Associates Center** (pp. 43-45) has a diamond-shaped roof, and the **Prudential Building** stands between that and the **Amoco Tower**. In front of the **Hancock Center** is **Water Tower Place** (p. 57), and to its right are **900 North Michigan Avenue**, and **Harbor Point** - this last part of the vast development near Lake Michigan known as the **Illinois Center**, not to be confused with the **State of Illinois Center** (pp.

28, 29) at Clark and Randolph Streets.

The twin towers of **Marina City** (p. 23), on the Chicago River, **444 North Michigan Avenue** near the Wrigley Building, the **Xerox Center** at 55 West Monroe, **333 West Wacker Drive** (p. 19), **Madison Plaza** (p. 39) built by the world-famous firm of Skidmore, Owings, and Merrill (which also built the Sears and Hancock Towers), the **IBM Regional Office** by Mies van der Rohe, the **Chicago Mercantile Exchange**, on South Wacker Drive (p. 27), and the residential complex of **Presidential Towers** on West Madison, are only a few of the many, many distinctive buildings which have been put up in Chicago in recent years. There is no way to describe them all or even name them, but a walk in Chicago's downtown will leave the visitor full of wonder and admiration at the quality, the quantity, and the beauty of most of these expressions of modern energy and taste.

For visitors who would like a more comprehensive guide to Chicago's modern architectural highlights, walking tours are available.

The **Art Institute of Chicago** (1892), one of the world's foremost museums.

Views past the Art Institute' **Lions** (1894) by Edward Kemeys, looking north along Michigan Ave.

The **Fountain of the Great Lakes** (1913) by Loredo Taft at the Art Institute, symbolically representing **Lakes Superior, Michigan, Huron, Erie** and **Ontario** - with water flowing from one to the other.

OLDER BUILDINGS

Older buildings of worldwide fame are the city's prestigious museums, built at the end of the last century when one of the greatest World Fairs was held in 1893 to commemorate Columbus... and Chicago, of course: the **World's Columbian Exhibition**. This enormous show occupied a 684 acre site south of the river and along the lake - now Grant and Burnham Parks.
In the few months of its existence it drew 21 million visitors - nearly twenty times the population of the whole city then. The **Art Institute** has been considerably expanded since its construction, the **Field Museum of Natural History** (p. 60), and the **Museum of Science and Industry** (p. 62), are all examples of the Neo-classic style of building which flourished at the end of the last century. Two other famous older

structures in Chicago are the **Merchandise Mart** (pp. 13, 18) on North Wells, once the largest commercial building in the world, and the Art Deco **Chicago Board of Trade Building** (p. 26) on West Jackson, both built in 1930.
But perhaps the most famous older structure of all is not a building but the **El** (p. 16), as the elevated train is called, which 'loops' round a section of the downtown area. This remaining elevated train was part of a vast steam and electric public transport system developed in the 19th and early 20th centuries, much of which has now disappeared or been replaced by buses. Chicago also has many surviving smaller residences and tenements built from before the turn of the century onwards, often with exterior fire escapes, a precaution resulting from the Great Fire (p. 17).

One of the most famous meeting places in Chicago is under the magnificent clocks on **Marshall Field's** on State Street.

TODAY'S CHICAGO

Today Chicago is one of the world's greatest metropolises. It's still, as it has been from its earliest moments, a crossroads. Today it is literally the world's greatest ground transportation crossroads. The routes that meet in Chicago are not only descendants of the vast water and rail arteries of the last century, but also the road and air ones of this. O'Hare airport is the world's busiest and, incidentally, maybe design-wise, the best. Together with Midway and Meigs airports, some sixty or seventy million people land or take-off every year. O'Hare alone handles well over fifty million passengers a year and some 800,000 flights, one every 40-45 seconds.

Chicago's a hub of all the spokes of transport for the center of the American continent, without equal. Chicago is near the centerpoint of population distribution in the United States; it's only about 150 miles north of the centerpoint of

Ornaments on the **Carson Pirie Scott Store** on South State St., by the famous Chicago architect Louis H. Sullivan.

industry; and of course it's near the center of the largest food-producing area in the world.

The enormous economic might of Chicago can be gauged by the statistic that in 1980 only eleven nations in the world had GNP's higher than Chicago.

Today it's a city of about 3 million people inside the Chicago city limits, and of about seven-and-a-half million people in the greater Chicago area, known as the **Chicago Standard Metropolitan Statistical Area** or SMSA. This consists of McHenry, Lake, Cook, DuPage, Kane and Will Counties in Illinois. The area within the Chicago city limits is 228 square miles more or less - comparable to the roughly 300 square miles within the New York city limits. The area of the SMSA is 4,653 square miles.

The population figures in 1980 for Chicago were about three million people and for SMSA about seven million people. Today, if the contiguous areas on Lake Michigan, in northern Indiana -

Gary, Hammond, and East Chicago - are included in the population of Chicago, the city might be as much as eight-and-a-half to nine million people.

The average annual temperature is about 51 degrees Fahrenheit. In the summer it can be hot - over 100 degrees F, - and in the winter, very cold, sometimes with a particularly nasty wind-chill factor. In the spring, summer and autumn weather is mostly mild and lovely, making watersports along the city's twenty-nine miles of shoreline one of Chicagoans' favorite pastimes. There are eight yacht harbors, in summer all packed with pleasure craft. Boats can be rented at many of these basins.

Chicago is also a city of parks - there are 574 of them - and of culture and education: there are twenty major museums and more than sixty art galleries.

Chicago has a world-famous symphony orchestra. There is the **Ravinia Music Festival** and also the

*Details from the **Chicago Theatre** (1921), on North State.*

One of the two-decker sightseeing buses, of the Chicago Motor Coach Co., which operate in warm weather. Passengers can join or leave the tour at a number of stages around the downtown area.

*Dawn Shadows (1982), the 30' high sculpture by Louise Nevelson at **Madison Plaza**, 200 W. Madison St.*

Chicago Lyric Opera. Popular music - particularly Jazz, Blues, and Country - can be heard in clubs and bars all over town. And of course many many national and international musical stars and groups hold concerts in Chicago all year round.

There are some fifty-eight colleges and universities, including many major medical establishments. Universities such as **Northwestern**, and the **University of Chicago** (p. 62), where Enrico Fermi's team of scientists produced the first controlled nuclear chain reaction in 1942, are of course among the best in the world. Many famous writers have lived or worked in Chicago: Carl Sandburg and Sherwood Anderson, Theodore Dreiser, Richard Wright, Hemingway, Saul Bellow, Studs Terkel and Edna Ferber are just a few of them. The spectrum of the city's literary output goes all the way from the **Encyclopedia Britannica** to **Playboy** magazine...

*The **First National Bank Building** and its Plaza, at Monroe and Dearborn.*

CHICAGO IN 1980

Chicago in 1980 was number one in the U.S. in steel production, with nine major steel plants, number-one in commercial printing, producing three-quarters of the nation's paperbacks, in appliance manufacture, in candy, in telephone equipment, in industrial machinery, in pots and pans, in diesel engines, railroad equipment, radios, TV's, sporting goods and in many, many other products.

It also leads the U.S. in foreign sales and in the mail order business.

Chicago is America's convention center, hosting some 1,500 of them, including trade shows, annually. It has, or had until very recently - so fast do new buildings go up - the world's tallest building (the **Sears**), the tallest bank (**First National**), tallest apartment and office building (**Hancock Center**), tallest apartment building (**Lakepoint Tower**) and tallest reinforced concrete building (**Water Tower Place**).

Chicago is about twenty-five miles from north to south and, at its widest, fifteen miles from the Lake westward, but the main section of the city is the downtown area to the north and south of the Chicago River and mostly to its east between the river and the Lake.

In the 'Loop', the area south of the Chicago River, State and Madison Streets are the dividing lines and building addresses are numbered from these.

*The skyline from Grant Park, including the **Sears Tower**, the **Encyclopedia Britannica Building**, the **Mid-Continental Plaza Building**, and the **Associates Center**.*

*Part of downtown Chicago seen through the spray of **Buckingham Fountain** (1927) - the **Associates Center** and the **Amoco Tower** are on either side of the fountain.*

Buckingham Fountain in Grant Park, one of the world's largest decorative fountains, dedicated in 1937.

North of the River downtown, Michigan Avenue is the main artery, running northwards through the downtown area until it merges with **Lakeshore Drive** along the **Gold Coast**, named for the considerable wealth of its inhabitants (p. 59). The Lake is always east in Chicago and the two most conspicuous north-south landmarks are both on it: **Grant Park** all along the Lake side of the 'Loop', and **Lincoln Park** at the north end of the Gold Coast.

Chicago is a city of neighborhoods. There are almost eighty of them and Chicagoans, when asked where they live, usually answer with a neighborhood name - Burnham Park, River City, West Loop, Lakeview, Edgewater, Hyde Park, Kenwood etc... The main divisions of the city are the **South Loop, Near Westside, North Lakefront, River North, Westside, South** and **Southwest Sides, North Westside**.

GETTING AROUND CHICAGO

Getting round Chicago is easy. Buses are excellent and transfers are available. The El, or elevated trains, and the subways are fast and efficient the former with wonderful vistas of the city. Taxis are everywhere but beware! - they charge for each passenger. Walking is a joy in Chicago, except of course when the north wind joins forces with the winter cold...

WHAT TO SEE IN CHICAGO

First of all there are the viewpoints, those at the top of the **Sears Tower** and the **John Hancock Center**. These views rival any from any building anywhere in the world.

Then there is a spectacular view from the Lake

Photo Gamma Chicago

Photo Gamma Chicago

43

*Views of the **Associates Center** from Grant Park.*

*The **Amoco Tower**, Chicago's third highest building, seen from Grant Park.*

towards the city either from **Navy Pier** or from private boats and sightseeing craft.

There is also a marvellous sunrise view to the east across the Lake, from most anywhere along Lakeshore Drive, or in Grant or Lincoln Parks. Then there are bus tours from the **Art Institute** at Michigan and Adams, as well as various coach tours of the city (p. 38), including ones which survey Chicago's architecture, particularly in the 'Loop', along the Gold Coast, at the various universities, and in Oak Park, ten miles west of downtown - where Frank Lloyd Wright worked. There are also organised walks among the architecture, the galleries, collections, and parks of the city, tailored for schools and private organizations, as well as walks through Oak Park. Two other attractions are **Here's Chicago**, a video tour of the city, and **Pullman Village**. Pullman was a company town - the company which made Pullman luxury railroad cars. The Pullman company owned everything - the housing, the stores, the entertainment, the utilities. Whatever the workers earned went back into the company by way of rent, movies utility bills. This area has been beautifully restored.

*The skyline from Grant Park, showing the **Encyclopedia Britannica Building.***

OTHER MODERN BUILDINGS TO BE SEEN

Besides the Sears and Hancock buildings, and the buildings already mentioned, some of the most popular are usually the **Daley Center Plaza** with its Picasso statue, **Lakepoint Tower, Lakeshore Drive Apartments**, by Mies van der Rohe, **Prentice Women's Hospital**, the **Swiss Grand Hotel, 33 West Monroe St., Three First National Plaza, Gateway IV, One Magnificent Mile**, the **Metropolitan Correctional Center, One and Two Illinois Center**, and the **Bloomingdale Building**.

MUSEUMS

Chicago's most popular museums are the **Art Institute**, the **Field Museum of Natural History** and the **Museum of Science and Industry**, all world-renowned museums. These three will each keep adults and children fascinated for many hours.

There are several other exceptional museums in Chicago, all very popular with visitors: the **Museum of Contemporary Art** shows what's happening in today's art world; the **Chicago Historical Society** shows Chicago's development with full-scale exhibits: the **Terra Museum of American Art** is an outstanding collection, mostly of 19th and 20th century drawings, watercolors, and paintings by Americans - Prendergast, Copley, Whistler, Homer, Morse and others; the **Du Sable Museum of African-American History** is one of the rare museums that tries to illustrate the enormous contribution to the United States of black Africans and of their culture. And the two university museums at **Loyola** - the **Martin d'Arcy** -, and at the **University of Chicago** - the **Smart** - show diverse art through the ages.

There are many other museums worth visiting. There is one, for example, which shows the contemporary and older art of the State of Illinois. There are others showing art from each of various ethnic groups - Mexican, Oriental, Polish, Lithuanian, Ukrainian, Swedish, and Jewish.

*Two views of Chicago's **Marina** on Lake Michigan.*

Following pages:
*the **Prudential** and **Amoco Buildings** from Lake Michigan; the tallest building in the world - the **Sears Tower** - dominates Chicago's skyline from Lake Michigan, with the Marina in the foreground, and the Marina, with **Harbor Point** on the left.*

KIDS AND YOUNG PEOPLE

Adler Planetarium is 'a must' for children. So is the **Chicago Academy of Sciences**, a natural history museum with fine exhibits, the **John G. Shedd Aquarium**, and the two wonderful **Zoos** in Brookfield and Lincoln Parks. Both the Police Department and the Fire Department, as well as the **American Police Center and Museum** provide tours illustrating their work, while the famed **Glessner House** has an exhibit of 19th century life for kids aged 6 to 10.

There's a one-and-a-half hour walking tour of the 'Loop' for kids and younger people, a tour of O'Hare Airport for them, a children's library, and special boat tours of the Chicago River and the Lake.

All the big museums have special arrangements for kids, especially the Art Institute which has a junior museum. There are also **Ripley's Believe it or Not** where the weird is normal, and the **Telephony Museum** with the history of the telephone. Two very special Chicago institutions which usually appeal to the young at heart are the **Farm-in-the-Zoo**, a five-acre working farm in Lincoln Park and the **Willowbrook Wildlife Haven** where sick and injured animals, reptiles and birds find refuge.

There are a number of eating places that cater for kids: **Choo Choo, Marshall Fields, Narcissus Room, Flukeys, Gertie's Ice Cream, Kaplan's** in Water Tower Place, and the **Halsted Fish Market**. Many libraries have Children's Rooms; and numerous art, dance, music and drama centers have special classes for them; sports centers abound, often with pools.

There are also lots of shops and displays of dolls and doll-houses, puppets, stuffed animals, comic books, trains and models, toys of all sorts, magic tricks, and a few children's theatres.

49

A magnificent twilight skyline vista of Chicago from Lake Michigan.

OTHER THINGS TO DO IN CHICAGO

The El. Take a ride on the El, particularly the **Ravenswood El** and look down on Chicago, up close.

Stock and Mercantile Exchanges. See the frenzied activity of America's commercial heart beat very, very fast.

Art Galleries. Walk in and out of these - there are many of them - just north of the Chicago River on West Erie, Huron and Superior, between Wells and Sedgwick.

Maxwell Street Market. The open-air flea market here is wonderful. It's near Halsted Street.

Cruises. There are various relaxing and spectacular sightseeing boats which offer trips on the Lake and along the Chicago River.

Here's Chicago! In the **Water Tower Pumping Station** on East Pierson just near Water Tower Place, in the only building still standing from the Great Fire of 1871, there's an informative audio-visual show outlining Chicago's yesterdays and its today. Beware, though, that when there are few tourists in town, the hours of the shows are erratic.

Arlington Raceway in suburban Arlington Heights is a must for lovers of horse-racing, easily accessible by commuter rail. Also worth while are **Foste** of Chicago, the **Air and Water Show**, and many local neighborhood festivals.

SHOPPING

Visit some of the most famous shops in the world, many of them native to Chicago. In particular **Carson Pirie Scott, Marshall Fields**, and **Montgomery Ward**. Also **Bonwit Teller, I Magnin, Lord & Taylor, Saks**, and **Neiman Marcus**. Water Tower Place's seven-storey gorgeous, glass atrium is amazing and wonderful - not to be missed. There's an atrium, too, in the **State of Illinois Center**, and a seven-level shopping center at the **Century** (pp. 28-29).
Others are **Ford City**, the **Brickyard** and **Harper Court**. Most of the famous boutiques and shops of the world have branches in these atriums and shopping centers.

But wandering up and down the main streets of downtown Chicago is the best shopping of all, the city's wide streets and wonderful vistas a magnificent backdrop to your wandering eye.

DINING AND ENTERTAINMENT

Chicago has some of the best food in America, especially meat. For three or four or five generations the **Chicago Stockyards** were the biggest and most famous in the world leaving a legacy of good meat which still infuses the city's

Two night-time views of Chicago's sparkling downtown from Lake Michigan.

*A night view of the **Michigan Ave Bridge** over the Chicago River.*

many restaurants.

And corn, of course, grows higher and better nearby than anywhere else in the world. So do wheat, barley, oats, and potatoes, and lots of other things as well.

So there's an established American habit of excellent food and friendly atmosphere, crossed with the long tradition of ethnic immigrant cooking: Chinese, Mexican, Middle Eastern, Polish, Czech, French, Greek, German, Italian, Hungarian, Ethiopian, Indian, Japanese, Vietnamese, Korean - you can find them all and lots more. Also **Cajun** - maybe the best Cajun food outside of Louisiana.

Blues are an absolute must in Chicago. And so is Jazz. Country, Bluegrass, Western, Reggae, Rock, Folk, Salsa, Gospel - it's all fabulous in Chicago. The canal from the Chicago River to the Des Plaines brought not only material wealth. It brought culture too. It meant that all the music of the West and the South, of the Appalachians, and of all the southwest with a Mexican influence, of

the Caribbean, and especially of New Orleans, drifted up stream to the mid-continent capital, Chicago. Jazz and Blues are so good you'll want to stay in town just to hear more.

Theatres. Traditionally the Chicago theatre consisted of out-of-town, mostly New York, work passing through. But now there are also innovative, original Chicago companies - some of the best in the country - over fifty theatres offering a wide range of classical and contemporary theatre.

Those offering comic improvisation and stand-up are especially wonderful. See the **Chicago Reader** to know what's going on in the Chicago theatre scene.

For a short time before Hollywood began Chicago was the film capital of America and there are still old movie houses to remind one of when film was king (p. 38). The influence of Canadian theatre too - very alive and active across the Great Lakes, especially in and around Toronto - is felt in Chicago.

PARKS, ARBORETUMS AND GARDENS

Although mostly flat and thus lacking many of the undulations of light and shade which hills bring, Chicago is nonetheless one of the great garden cities of the world, often compared with London in this respect.

Besides the Lakeshores and beaches, there are botanical gardens, conservatories, arboretums, forest reserves, nature centers and trails galore. And of course to the north, along Lake Michigan and in Wisconsin, there's open-country and a water wonderland. The main city parks are **Burnham, Douglas, Garfield, Grant, Humbolt, Jackson, Kenwood, Lincoln, McKinley, Midway Plaisance, Olive, Peterson, Union, Washington** and **Wicker**: these together total almost 4,000 acres of park with every facility imaginable. There are besides twenty botanical gardens, conservatories and arboretums, as well as nine major forest preserves in Cook County alone, into which no cars are permitted - only walking, hiking, bicycling, and horseback riding, together with swimming in the summer and skiing in the winter.

Chicago is one of the world's great business and pleasure cities. It's a city to visit and to enjoy. We hope you return many times and on each visit discover more of the endless charm and fascination of CHICAGO!

*Two views of the **Water Tower** on North Michigan at Chicago, the only public building to withstand the Great Fire of 1871.*

A view across Chicago showing the **Amoco Tower**, and in the distance the **Hancock Tower**. The many ground level parking lots which seem so strange in the downtown area of tall buildings will probably one day all be sites for Chicago's skyscrapers of the future.

Looking north towards the **Hancock Tower** and Lake Michigan. On the left is the **Bloomingdale Building**, the towers of which are beautifully lit at night. **Water Tower Place** is the tall building to the right of the **Hancock**.

Looking north along **Lake Shore Drive** and Lake Michigan towards Lincoln Park, and Evanston. In the lower half of the photo is Chicago's famous **Gold Coast** - named for the wealth of its inhabitants.

SPORTS

Sports are a very big thing in Chicago and the names of the teams are municipal and national treasures. 'Being a Cub fan is one of the greatest things you can do with your life', a Chicagoan once said about his love of baseball and how the Cubs play it... Besides the **Cubs**, at Wrigley Field and the **White Sox** at Comiskey Park, there are the **Bears** of football at **Soldier Field** (p. 61), the **Bulls** of basketball, and the **Black Hawks** of ice hockey at Chicago Stadium.
There are also collegiate teams - Northwestern, Loyola, Chicago State, University of Illinois at Chicago, and the University of Chicago. Sometimes, like it should be, these teams are great, sometimes they aren't...

Chicago is the site for **America's Marathon**, a running race, the **Golden Gloves Boxing Tournament**, the **MacMurray Basketball Tournament**, and the **Mackinac Sailboat Race**. Sailing is a wonderful pastime on Lake Michigan, (pp. 48-54), as is motor-boating, windsurfing, canoeing, water-skiing etc... And if you feel you're good enough you can sail all the way across the five Great Lakes and then up the Saint Lawrence to the Atlantic. Swimming is great in the Lakes too but they say the Saint Lawrence rapids are too much for most swimmers...
There are thirty-one **Park District** beaches open from June 15th to September 15th, meaning that during those months the city provides them with lifeguards, as well as **Wilmette Beach, Illinois State Beach State Park**, and the **Indiana Dunes**.

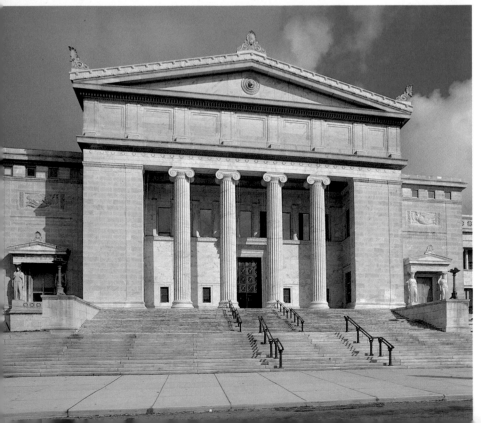

The **Field Museum of Natural History** -
anthropology, botany, geology and
zoology - grew from Chicago's 1893
World's Columbian Exhibition. One of
the world's greatest museums -
containing some 13 million artifacts.

You can find archery, badminton, billiards, bowling, biking, balooning, caving, cricket, croquet, darts, fencing, fishing (lots and lots of it, but you need a licence), also ice-fishing, flying, golf, horseback riding, skating, lawn-bowling, bocce, racquet ball, rugby, skeet shooting, skiing, sky-diving, softball, tennis, tobogganing, and volleyball - all in Chicago.

Soldier Field in Grant Park, home of the Chicago Bears football team, originally built as a war memorial.

Harper Memorial Library at the **University of Chicago**, Midway Plaisance near East 59th Street. The statue is of the Swedish Botanist Carolus Linneaus (1707-1778) the originator of our system for naming plants.

Rockefeller Chapel at the University of Chicago, built in 1928. Its 72-bell carillon of chimes rings every quarter hour.

Museum of Science and Industry in Jackson Park, one of Chicago's most popular attractions and one of the world's finest museums. It has many extraordinary exhibits, created to engage the visitor directly in modern technology.

Loredo Taft's 1922 enormous and moving monument, **The Fountain of Time**, contains a mass of volatile humanity set across a pool from the unmoving figure of Time. One of Chicago's many public sculptures, it stands in **Washington Park** at the western end of the Midway Plaisance.

INDEX